'Nadine Aisha Jassat captures the nuances and complexities of mother/daughter relationships so beautifully in this collection. Her poetry is a vivid exploration of what it means to be somewhere in the inbetween, and how we make homes in the stories that anchor us. Her voice is extraordinary and fearless and compelling, a must read.'

– Shagufta K Iqbal (*Jam is for Girls)*

'A dazzling and deft debut collection that will carousel around the psyche for many moons. These poems ooze into you, into readers of every ilk, asking worthy questions of themselves and the world beyond – here be words lighting fuses.'

– Michael Pedersen (*Oyster*)

'An important collection of poems, incisive, delicate and precise, as it interrogates the trauma of systemic and every day racism. Jassat is unflinching as she delivers lyrical gut punches that stay with you for days.'

– Nikesh Shukla (*The One Who Wrote Destiny*)

'There is so much beauty and truth in these verses … The book itself is a journey, an exploration, an invitation even, to reflect on the way we navigate this patriarchal, racist, postcolonial world.'

– Zeba Talkhani (*My Past is a Foreign Country*)

'Have you read Nadine Aisha? If not, you're seriously missing out. She kicks serious arse.'

– Kirsty Logan (*The Gracekeepers*)

LET ME TELL YOU THIS

NADINE AISHA JASSAT

Published by 404 Ink

www.404Ink.com

@404Ink

Opening quote is from *Borderlands/La Frontera: The New
Mestiza.* Copyright © 1987, 1999, 2007, 2012 by Gloria
Anzaldúa. Reprinted by permission of Aunt Lute Books.
www.auntlute.com

ISBN: 9781912489121

ebook ISBN: 9781912489138

Editor: Shagufta K Iqbal

Cover illustration: Shazleen Khan

Typesetting: Laura Jones

Printed and bound in Great Britain
by Clays Ltd, Elcograf S.p.A.

CONTENTS

HANDS

WORDS

VOICE

'I will have my voice... I will overcome...'

Gloria Anzaldúa, *How to Tame a Wild Tongue*

HANDS

LIFE IN THE UK

with thanks to Talat Yaqoob

You keep your head down, frown
and don't say anything

while the man on the tube
places his gaze on you
like stones:

your hands, your child, your language,
your clothes
mustn't grumble

as your colleagues joke,
their mouths laughing fake accents
(which keep yours shut) they boast

about their Indian on a Friday night,
drink from yellow and purple mugs, and you

keep out of sight

when the country is reeling,
and you, too, are grieving
yet asked to apologise

by politicians in suits who tighten their ties
with one hand, the other
gripping a pen which hovers and signs

an X over your headscarf, over your mother
tongue, and you

don't say anything,

you know if you try, they'll only Prevent you
yet, when you step outside,
the kids

at the back of the bus,
street corner, shop door and school
call you Paki cunt, Muslim bitch, terrorist, cruel

tea is served, pale brown and well brewed
steam rising up to heaven
whether thrown down your back
or steeping, gently,
beside your prayer mat.

THIRD GENERATION

After Langston Hughes' 'Cross'

My old man's a brown old man,
and my old mother's white.
When they ask if he's from Pakistan,
I'm told to be polite.
When they say she's not my Mother,
I say to me we look the same,
and when they tell me to be ashamed of them,
I say I have two worlds to gain.
My Bali wants a suburban house
to prove himself to you,
and if my Ma ever left that house
you'd condemn him for that too.
I grew myself from both of them
each bone, each nail, each tooth.
I wonder how my children will grow,
under the shadow of this roof?

THE OLD CODGERS

My parents' mouths pull at the corners of my mine,
a tug I'll share with yours if I try sing to their tune.

My father's is a dance;
of Hindi-meets-Shona-meets-Gujarati-meets-Afrikaans,
where a woman is a *honey*, a child a *lytie*
and heaven help you if you hear *voetsak, cutri,* or *woe*.
I grew up fluent in the tightened jaw
of the Old Bali on the phone: 'Hallo,
this is Mr Jassat speaking,'
his accent so-suddenly English,
from a county we've never visited,
never mind own.

My mother, all Yorkshire, all drawn out vowels,
calls a poem a *poym*, and greets Auntie
with a rounded mouth
and the India of her mind
pressing on her tongue.
Releases each sentence as a question,
punctuated by an outside laugh

that makes me want to ask,
who it is when it's at home.

And I? I say *owt* and *nowt* and *sommet* and *innit*.
I say *Litchi* not *Lychee*, *Samoosa* not *Samosa*,
and *Aye,* and *Arse,* and *Loo* and *Snicket*.
Bath is never *Baaath*, *Room* is never *Ruhm*.
When I greet you, I may say, 'Now, then,'
just like my Mum.
And when I leave you,
I may say, 'As Salaam Alaikum.'

MY THREE EARLIEST MEMORIES OF MY FATHER

1.

Toddler tiny, high chair
I sit – strawberry-mush-handshakes,
and baby giggles.
He, across the room from me,
is taking my brother to the Fair.
I am too small.

2.

Playground. Knee high socks
and gingham. School bell sounding
and children running, screaming,
joy. He appears, at the gates, tall,
suited, booted, strong afro.
The space around him is empty.

3.

Face to face, he kneels,

looks me in the eye, and says:

'When they call you a Paki, tell them,

"Oh, have you been? I hear it

is a beautiful country."'

PAKI HANDS

After applying her fake tan,
she says, 'Look, I've got Paki hands,'
and I turn into myself
for a breath.

I've never been to Pakistan,
but I have held 'Paki' in my hands;
scraped it off my shoulders
the curves of my chest
brought it back here,
laid it to rest.

I could ask her what she means,
but then I'd be told I'm making a scene.
But if I stay quiet – gaze lowered
to pale-dark hands, feet, and knees –
what will that silence do to me?

She places down the bottle,
wipes her palms clean, and leaves.

By the time her 'Paki hands' fade
to white, I promise myself I will decide,
what I'm going to do with mine.

HOLIDAY SNAPS

Cape Town, 2017

Her hands appear in every picture,
though she refuses to let me capture her face,
cries of 'too old,' 'my lipstick', 'my expression',
making a selfie something she always evades.

So instead I settle for a thumb and forefinger,
pointing at some wonder far away,
or her wedding band, hands held just so,
waiting to cut cake.

Whichever way you look at it,
landscape or portrait,
there's a wrist with seven gold bracelets
in the foreground of every picture I take.

Last night I found an eclipse of brown,
obscuring all but a sliver of the frame.
Fingerprints so close they blur,
this is how I capture her,
in the snaps from my holiday:

11

mountains and adventures,
and flowers and feasts and planes,
and Auntie, always Auntie,

Auntie never far away.

COMMITTEE MEETING

We are organising a festival
for BME women. We will
call it: 'Women of the World
in Scotland.' We have
asked representatives from
the Jewish and African and
ethnic communities. There
will be a Chinese lady
doing calligraphy, there
will be an exhibition of
dressmaking from
Palestine (but no talk, so
as not to be political), we
are organising a festival
for BME women and we'll
do a 'Salwar Kameez' swap,
if that's what you call it,
and hope it's ok to stick pins
in the fabric on display.
It will be so beautiful
our very own festival
of BME women

polished brown skin
behind sharp boxed glass.

BUILT TO LAST

'The ancient Egyptian civilization lasted for over 3,000
years. Most of the evidence that survives today comes
from temples and tombs that were built to last.'
— As recorded in the poet's notes,
from The British Museum signage, 2017.

1. Entrance

You old, colossal, colonial thing.
At one turn a marvel of the world.
At another, a treasure grabbing fiend.

I remember you from childhood.
Six to sixteen, I was fascinated:
Ancient Rome, Egypt, Maya, Greece.

Scrawled my name in hieroglyphs,
convinced I'd mastered an ancient language
translated from a tacky souvenir of yours,
my own Rosetta stone.

Curled up, I explored the stories
of Horus, Hatshepsut, Sekhmet,
with a papyrus book mark
that I'd suck as I read
absorbed
until it left itself
salt white
on my tongue,
my stomach aching.

I am not a child anymore,
as I stand at your door
and stare at the statue of Ramses' head
eyes fixed on the bullet hole in his breast
the crack across his middle
deep as the earth.

Here is a story I was never told,
but I have returned to ask.
Here is a story, ancient and old,
that was built to last.

2. Acquisition

I seek out my favourite object of all,
a statue I remember from when I was too small
to read the imprint on her case.
The letters sink in my mouth like a stone;
the name of an army man,
by which she is known,
no sign of her howl, her spirit, her soul,
only *hollow cast; seated cat;*
inlaid; incised;* treasured find.

I do not know the language for this.
Can't picture the hieroglyphs, birds, snakes and reeds
which you'd told me was all that I would need
to begin to unlock the past.

I'm starting to learn your ways,
through your attitude to names.
Stories untold, makers' hands forgotten
once the item is marked 'sold' (or 'gifted', never stole–)

Hm. Don't forget. You're supposed to be a Brit.
We don't talk about this.

---

*   *Quoted directly from an exhibit description.*

17

We don't talk,
about this general of war,
who landed a goddess not his on this shore,
who gave her his name
like a weight, chipped away
at her gleam, and painted her green.
Shoved a rod up her back,
repaired a crack
(or so you claim it to be)
and 'donated' her here,
circa 1930.

Never mind that she was made
in 600 BC.

Never mind that you don't say
how she came to be.

It's in those years, so tactfully removed
that I find where you hide, masked now behind
your version of the truth, glass cases,
and clacking keyrings.

3. Thank You For Visiting

I have returned to the ancestors with a scream.
Half held in the turn of my jaw.
The pin pricks behind my eyelids.

There's a weight to my echo,
in your cool marble halls,
as it considers the price of all this taking
and remaking yours.
I circle the general, circle the cat,
write down the words 'built to last',
and wonder
which will be the first to go.

Meanwhile, among these endless floors,
people of all nations pulse,
faces reflected in what's on display.
And rows of boxes, opaque grey,
placed in prime position,
ask us to donate.

Perhaps the question I'm asking is:
who am I among all this?
Worshipper, Returner, Tourist, Hypocrite?
African, Indian, Arab, British?

Truth Teller, Word Spinner, Poet, Activist?
And who are you, but one cog in the machine
onto whom I project my grief?

But really, is it a projection at all,
for when evening comes
you still close your doors.

CONVERSATIONS
AS GIRLS

'Nadine,

how come you're so pale?'

'Nadine,

you are so lucky, you have

the best of both worlds:

Muslim skin   and   English voice.'

'Nadine,

how come you're so pale?'

'It must be hard,

being mixed race.'

'Nadine,

are you Muslim or Christian?

I know

most girls

follow

after their mothers.'   'See, all these white girls,

who go out with brown men –

                                        it's fashionable.'

                'Nadine,

                how come you're so pale?'

'I'm glad my parents are the same

                                        – Pure Blood.'

                'Nadine,

                you have to be

one or   the other,'

                'Nadine,

do you have the same Dad

                                        as your brother?'

                'Nadine,

you don't really look

                                        like your Mother',

'You've got

                your Father's

                                        'colouring."

22

'Nadine,

how come you're so pale?'

'It must be hard,

being mixed race.'

'Half–

Caste'   'Na

dine,

you are

so lucky.

You have   the best

of both worlds:

Muslim skin   and   English voice.'

'Muslim skin   and   English voice',

and English voice

and English voice

and English voice

'And,

how do   I   pronounce it

again?'

'Could you spell

your surname   again

       for   me,

                        Nadia?'

       'Nadine,

    you have to be one

           or the other

   you can't be nothing.'

      'Nadine –

where are you from?'

    'Where's that?'

THINGS I WILL TELL MY DAUGHTER

If I have a daughter I will tell her
that there are some things
which people will tell you as truth.
Don't believe them.

I'M NOT RACIST, I'VE GOT A MIXED RACE KID

Her mother's skin is brown.
Shade 242, Honey Bronze Sunset,
to be precise.

It comes out of a bottle,
the way so much of her does:
   hair comes out,
     nails come out,
      skin comes out,
a ragged motley costume.

It's easier to define than what she puts back in:
the words underneath
'we don't talk about that,'
sneering faces,
first kisses
and how it felt
aged 13,

the first time she knew
her body had to change.
Her father's razor;
her legs;
a pattern of nicks from the blade.

She passes it on.
Conformity looks a lot more like safety
when wrapped in a bikini.
Better not to stand out
for the wrong reasons.

Out on the beach,
downscaling sun factors by the day,
she looks at her daughter and I hear her say:
'What a lovely colour you are.'
'You've turned such a wonderful brown.'

I wonder if the daughter notices
the oddity of the grammar,
as her mother proclaims jealousy,
and then looks at me,
somewhere between board shorts
and burkini,
        a warning
not to take it too far.

'What a lovely colour you are.'

I wonder what her daughter thinks,
about 'turning brown'.
I wonder if her daughter's brown
is shaped like a country,
or has its own smell;
chopped coriander, chai, sadza, rice.

If someone has already told her
to pick sides.

If she has yet learned shame,
and which half came first;
Don't be like them,
  Don't follow her,
    You're like us,
     Those people aren't safe
      That's not your place.
I wonder if the comb stuck in her hair, too.

    Maybe her dad is a story that starts and ends
        with the syllable men.
      Maybe her dad isn't her dad.
      Maybe her dad is the man she shouts at.

Maybe her dad swapped his accent for a safer one.
Maybe her dad may be her Dad.
It's rude of me to ask.

Still,
I look at her, she looks at me,
and while her mother's words build
like clouds above;

'I'm not a racist,

but – '

I want to slow the world
to just her and me,
ask:

does she say you don't need
all the things she doesn't want you to be?

Family, community, oils, spices, recipes?

Does she tell you it's a compliment
when people ask where you're from?

Does she say she wishes she looked so exotic,
then smirks at women in kurtas and chitenge?

Does she buy the wrong shampoo?
Does it take to your hair like salt,
drawing you out from the root?

When you come home from school,
scratched knees and broken words in your head,
a drum beaten question,
does she call the racists 'bullies'?

Does she call it race at all,
or does she tell you she doesn't see it?

Does she say;
    don't fuss,
        look here,
her skin is brown, too.
Honey   Bronze   Sunset.

Aren't you both the same?

OR,

You should stay out of the sun, beta.
Such lovely, white, skin.

SCOT-MID

I am 26,
walking through quiet Edinburgh streets
on my way to the supermarket.

There's a shopping list in my head, chanting
aubergine – ginger – butter to make ghee –
aubergine – ginger – butter to make ghee.

Two children trail in front of me,
at the tail coats of fathers
who walk further ahead
in heavy laced boots.
The wee boy turns,
I smile, he screams.
He screams,
'You're a bad woman!'

His sister hushes him away, apologetic.
Tells me he didn't mean it.
I am panic: eyes to the child,
to the pavement, to the wall,
did anyone else hear?

To the pavement, to the wall,
did anyone else hear him?
To the child, to the floor.

Returning home,
conscious of my face in that child's mind
and the newspapers he has seen
and the television he has watched
and the words he has heard,
I have a memory, briefly,
of a university friend
in consoling tones
telling me
I could 'pass for white'.

No matter how gentle.
No matter how serene.
No matter how many good works I do,
or taxes I pay,
or lives I save,
I will always be,
always be, to them
a dangerous woman.

And what are they to me?

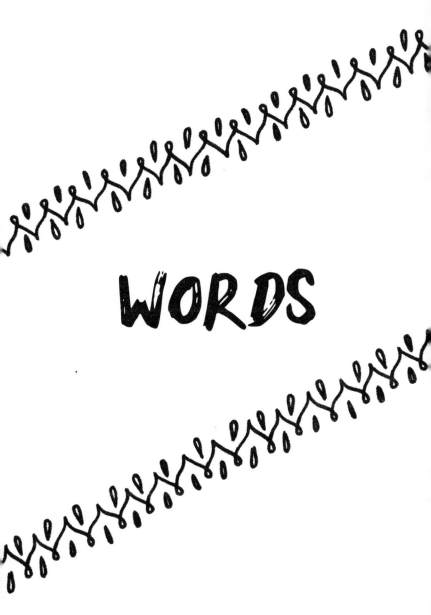

WORDS

MOTHER

He told me not to heed the Old Wives' Tales,
superstition and elaboration
bound in proverb and fable.

At home, by the kitchen table,
I watch my mother's hands spin the yarn
of meals and housework,
of duty and obligation.

I long to hear the tales in you.
To know that self beyond dinner time and bedtime,
to know the time of the tick of your heart,
which echoes in mine.

I wish I could press my ear to you like a shell,
to hear the ocean of you,
to know the roar that is yours.

What if it gets washed away too quickly?
And I live my life without your tales –

Searching, in the empty space by the kitchen table,
in the silence, for the words which were my mother.

MOTHER'S DAY

You came for a weekend trip.
Travelled North from chores and children,
lunches to be packed, beds to be pressed, and I
couldn't help but notice,
you didn't really leave them behind.

The ring of your phone, your laugh
not really a laugh at all. You tell me
you don't know why they bother,
when they say all you ever do is moan.

There's a bitterness in you I want to quell and free
like marbles spilling from nets and hands.
And a loneliness I cannot offer a comfort to,
without moving back and you
would never hold me to that. Love

is strange – when the child becomes the mother,
and the mother   sits, across from me,
in her hands a poorly wrapped token
of affection, the card too pink, too generic,

as if the word 'Mum' could ever capture the sum
of those care-worn hands, that hard gentle face.

INHERITANCE

She calls it having a word with herself.
My mother, looking at me,

saying all the things she needs
and doesn't.

Fear does what it is supposed to,
to hold you tight,

until a word with yourself is the only way
you can try to pause the descending,

spiralling, tapping, trapping
paralysis but for the beating fist;

What if? But then? If I don't? If I do?
Anxiety. 4 syllables given to this ceaseless, connecting string.

This genetic-chemical-taught-inherited
threaded parallel between

My mother and me.

My mother and me.

Threaded parallel between
this genetic-chemical-taught-inherited

Anxiety. 4 syllables given to this ceaseless, connecting string.
What if? But then? If I don't? If I do?

Paralysis but for the beating fist
spiralling, tapping, trapping.

You can try to pause the descending,
until a word with yourself is the only way

to hold you tight.
Fear does what it is supposed to,

and doesn't.
Saying all the things she needs,

My mother. Looking at me.
She calls it having a word with herself.

THREADS

At first, we thought it wasn't as bad as all that;
        everyone forgets with age,
                        and my Grandmother
        always did have a taste
                      for the dramatic.

Now, over telephone static,
           your voice   fades
as fast as your memory,
        threads of   who
               you
                 were
offered to me,
thin as loose cotton
        stray
from the weave
and spiralled on your overcoat.

Our conversations are limited.
I can't ask you what you did
             Yesterday
or even this morning.

Instead, I look for something to bind
whatever you are able to bring
to   mind:
        looping it like ribbon
        around the time
between
        your thoughts arriving,
and
        leaving again.

Today, that talk is dressmaking.
which is somehow also   your Mother,
        and the sense that you think
        I'm your   daughter.
                I wait for you
        to call me by her name.

I don't know how to dressmake,
but if I could, I'd sew a quilt
with patches of the way
        the women
in my Mother's   family
all wear the same face,
        and I don't.

Something in my lips
has been   unstitched
from this pattern
of   Collins women
(or is it Hinton, or Udall,
or Emery?).
Maiden names made un-chained,
 and hidden in the seams.

          The author
who could rewrite this   invisibility:
          my Grandmother.
Instead, she is busy,
          discovering a secret no-one else knows;
          how to return
          to youth,
                    how to bring
                    the dead   back
                    to life.

          How to conquer time.

Until it's me who is caught behind.

Gathering frayed ends.
Trying to follow

the chalk of her
                line,
        as the   present slips
                so far ahead
                    that the moth bitten   past
                is all that we have   left
                to see.

        And me.

Trying to use my words
like stitches.
Afraid that without them,
we'll both be   lost.

And all I'll have is memories,
        and cloth:

        the itch of wool
against my skin
        that you once held and shaped,
now resting gently
on my frame;
        your needles clicking,
        your hands precise,

your voice
reminding me
how to hold my tension,
how to position my bias across the line,

how to make something beautiful.
Something useful.
From   tangled yarn
          and threads.

Everywhere I look,
I find things I have inherited.

Perhaps I'll gather this too.
Perhaps I've already begun
                    to unspool
               and make
               my journey
                    through time.

                         Maybe there
                         I'll meet your fingers
                         and join your thumb
                         with mine.

Measure the distance
as if it were a simple bolt,
across which our two hands
now span.

A poem for your thoughts.
A knitted jumper,
made in the same way.

Threads
meeting
threads
meeting
threads
meeting
threads.

Picking up
where we left
off.

AFTER

for Bawa.

After dinner, we sat on the veranda,
and in between the creak of the swing,
and the song of the crickets,
you told me I'd shown you what happiness was.

I smiled in response, awkward, British,
unused to feelings spoken,
unused to silences which invited rather than ignored.

I didn't know then that your words would fill silences
I hadn't yet heard.

They filled the space between our hands as we parted.
They filled border checks and airports,
and miles, and seas, and lands, and homes.

Now there's time inbetween us.
There's dust and there's life
and there's *I'll never see you again.*

And there's the creak of the veranda swing.
There's the crickets, and the heat,
and the motion beneath me,
as we rock back and forth,
filled with your words.

AUNTIE

My Aunt's hands are soft and brown
and they smell like cumin and coriander.
She is a gardener in the kitchen.

Auntie, I remember your skin
the way some people remember the bus route.
I know I need to trace it to go home.

The world of work, bus bells and sirens
are harsh alarm clocks.
I would rather wake gently,
in 5 am light,
to your softly whispered duas
welcoming the morning.

THE GIFT

The trick is to post things that won't be missed:

a Bollywood film, knock off
from cheap corner stores. *Rylands*
and a reminder, of a tongue that you don't speak.

Socks, from our winter
to your summer.
The solstices of longest
and shortest
always falling on the same day

for you – two *Fizzlers*,
your favourite childhood treat.
You are grown now,
so with it we send Masala chai,
one sachet, unsweet.
You can add your own Scottish sugar,
if you need.

And on the back:
a return address,
in case it gets lost
in transit

between us, our names
front and back, either way
this gift will always find its way
home.

GIRL TIME

And so, the time came to go through her jewellery,
the last of it
the little bits,
we can't let go.

We were told
that anything of value was sold,
and what's left didn't matter.

> I wanted to hold your hand at the funeral
> but I couldn't find the right time.

You said,
'let's do it together
come down for some "girl time",
just you and me.'

I don't know what was worse,
seeing her handwriting, or holding
what was hers, feeling
as if we could meet in her last touch,
and go our parting ways.

I can't remember when we last spoke,
and that is a betrayal.

I read the addresses on the jewellery boxes,
forming a map in my mind.
Her story is told here:
Doncaster, Sheffield, Darwin,
Southport, Newquay, Darwin,
Darwin, Darwin, *Darling*.
That's what she used to call me.
I've kept them all, empty boxes and costume pearls
and the growing weight of words, words, words.

We made two piles:
yours, and mine.
Both hers, or at least were.
We didn't know what to do
with her husband's watches –
a surprise really, that she kept them –
they sit inbetween us, and not one of them ticks.
Caught up in the moment,
        I miss you
putting your findings away.
Upstairs dense footsteps creak,
men rising – yours, and mine,
but I don't want to let go of girl time,

of all that is still left.

I wonder if I'll see those pearls again,
the ones that you have kept,
in my own collection someday.
      Hush, now.
It feels too heavy
to think of you that way.

BRAIDS

'I live in a brown land which is turned and tilled ...
Brown is much maligned'
Michael Morpurgo, on the British landscape

'Now listen', is how her stories start,
recipe and rhyme.
'Now listen.'

1986

Fingerprints are colourless
left on the car window.
Her hands are russet
woods and story spinners that I remember.
On cold glass they are markers
of the distance inbetween.

Outside two children stare.
You touch your headscarf lightly.

1996

We stop the car for photos, often.
This is the Old Queen's parade,
her victory tour through the grand UK.
Though hand gestures in the street are unwelcome Vs.

She says she doesn't care for the cold,
then smiles gently at amber mittens,
folded in her lap.

2014

I have that smile too –
I tucked it between the folds of your sari,
under Auntie's spare bed.

Now I can count the places I feel close to you
on these very hands which came from you.

I make a mess when rolling rotis.
Flour in all the creases.

2011

On a polaroid left with your things,
Glencoe sweeps like a wave frozen into the land.
Beneath it an annotation;
'England, 1986.'
I don't know what to make of this.

Present

A hazel colour palate,
almond and mahogany,
brown is what you gave to me –
is the cool special
of your cinnamon spiced hands
and my sable hair.
Softly, they rest
at the nape.

EMBROIDERIES

Auntie sent a table runner from South Africa,
hand embroidered.

Auntie, you left the pins in –
they caught my fingers in the unwrapping.

Look here, can you see the marks?

SAM

1. *Sameer* (with the emphasis on the end: *meer*) is a Muslim name for boys. We are told it means companion, in particular one who stays up late talking and entertaining others, also known as a storyteller.

2. The poet's grandmother and her grandmother's sister, both famous in the family for their stories, were called Fatima Ali Bin Mahomed (later Jassat upon marriage) and Aisha Ali Bin Mahomed. The poet and her brother are both named to honour these storytelling sisters: Nadine Aisha Jassat, and Sameer Ali Bin Mahomed Jassat.

3. When asked how the poet's brother spells the 'Mahomed' in his name, he replies: 'Ma-home-d'. *My home.*

He asked us to call him Sam.
Cut off his ear so the name we would hear
was this: 3 letters. 2 syllables. One word.
Fits on a keychain. Fits on a form. Fits in.

Sameer. If you say it fast,
mouth lazy and half shut,
it sounds like the long thick mark
laid against us,
our names, our faces, our skin.

71

Smear.

Sam*eer*. If you give it time, say it slow
and let it grow – each letter allowed its own space
in your mouth which opens wide, like a greeting
you could almost be forgiven for hearing
SameerSameerSamheereSamehere Same Here.

'We have far more in common than that which divides.'

Yet your name is split.
Straight down the middle
your letters two islands of three
amid the silent sea that I too
have crossed. Sam   eer
that last lost syllable calls me here, here.
Here.

Littlest brother.
6ft3 and yet to me you will always be
that scrawny bundle of 7 years old,
sat on the floor of an airport lounge
spelling out the letters on your passport,
each sound a question;
'Ah – Luh – Ih - Buh – Ih – Nuh – Muh – Ah – Huh –
Oh – Muh – Eh – Duh'.

A pause.

And then:
'I've got five names and one of them's Bin!'
So, we called you 'Wheelie',
and joked
 if you wanted to go to America,
you wouldn't get in.

Sam. Sameer Ali Bin Mahomed Jassat.
My name ends where yours begins
a family tree held between you and me
on paper.
Stories passed down.
Stories remembered in our names.
Don't shorten them now.
Don't tell half the tale.

VOICE

HOPSCOTCH

'Alright tight pants?'

He says to me.

I am 16.

    'I like the way you wear that

                      piece.'

I am 23.

    'Nice puss ** **.'

I am not a cat.

    'Yowsa!'

        'Hey beautiful – '

          'Isn't she

               Gorgeous

                  Stunning

                     Bollywood Babe

                        I want you.'

Sat on the bus with a strangers' hot breath –

    'I want you.'

I still feel his heat in my ear when I hear,

    'Sexy'

        'Pretty'

            'Beautiful'

'Fit'

'Stuck Up Bitch'

'I'd give her one.'

'What's wrong?'

'Can't you take this?'

'It's just a compliment?'

'Where's your boyfriend?'

'What's your name?'

'Darling, I'd – '

No

'Has anyone ever told you,

you look like Nicole Scherzinger?'

'Has anyone ever told you

you're beautiful?'

Has anyone ever told you

they don't stop

telling me.

They're paving my streets with cobbles –

'Are you Spanish?'

'Are you Greek?'

'Do you speak Iranian?'

'Oh,

You're just another sunbed addict.'

No.

I'm tripping as I walk on
        'But your hair,
                but your eyes,
                        but your skin,
                                but you don't look Scottish,
                                        and where,
                                    where,
                            where are your family from,
                                originally.'
How I wish –
        'How I wish I had your tan!'
                'Is your Dad in the Taliban?'
                        'You should go back home now,'
                            'go back home,'
                                    'go back to – '
Where?
        'Your Mum.'

                        'Your Mum's a Paki lover.'
I am 14.

                                    'Slut.'
She was 43.

                                    'Slag.'
This isn't just me.

These words, they're like Tuesdays,
there's one every week.

I've held them between pressed palms
and Yale locks.

Consulted them like a guidebook
to my own hometown.

Clenched them tight in fists
that now mark the imprint of nameless men
trying to name me.

I stare hard at hands and fists and feet
don't walk don't look don't think don't be –
that key in my hand turning a lock in my throat – don't
feel another man's teeth as I walk these streets
of you and me, yet
I exist, somewhere between
   'are you Asian?'
             and
                'Nice tits!'
And let's just name the problem here:
these streets I've walked I've walked in fear,
and never once have these words begun
in a woman's mouth.

Still,

I'm leaving them here.

COIN TOSS

In response to a One Penny Coin, branded with 'Votes for Women' on the head of the King, held at Glasgow Women's Library's Suffragette archive.

1. Heads

12th November, 1910

I say, you think you can tax so much of my wage
but then won't give me a say on how it gets paid?
I say, it's not *my* law
which makes the roof over my head
more my husband's than mine;
nor that disavows me from quitting the swine
at a time of my own choosing.
A penny from my thoughts
meets a penny in my fist.
Friday next, me and my Sis
will make our mark,
not just on money but in minds:
Deeds Not Words, till the end of my days.
Votes for Women. That's what I say.

2. Tails

6th February, 2018

I saw it online; women fighting head to tail for their rights.

Retweet: #votesforwomen #metoo

#timeforchange #changestartswithyou.

The thing is, there's still so much to do:

women face violence every day,

are taxed on tampons, denied equal pay, even get scoffed at

if we save our own names for our children.

When you tell me we've won equality,

I'll tell you at least two of my sisters are murdered a week

by men. We're at a coin toss in history,

spinning in the air between how far we've come,

and where we need to be. I've heard the tales,

I'll take them with me, as I use my words in protest.

As I forge ahead. As we forge ahead.

SOPHIE

'Such a fine sunny day, and I have to go'

– from the last words of Sophie Scholl, age 21, who was part of the
White Rose resistance group, distributing anti-fascist literature.
She was executed by Nazi Germany for her role in the resistance.

Such a fine sunny day, today
and I have to go

out and against the terror
which every minute slowly grows;

to alter minds already formed,
and teach those that are new,

whether its pamphlets made by my hand,
or placards made by you.

To give myself to stories,
shared, spoken, heard.

To use my voice against the odds;
to change the odds with every word.

Still, the challenges only seem to get higher,
every day brings something new.

And though we expect more struggles to come,
it's still a cold grief when they do.

What I'd give for this to be the last one;
for generations to remember, but never truly *know*.

Such a fine sunny day, today.
And I have to go.

BITE

Coming to, I was confused.
The bed beneath me not the forest floor
I'd seen coming into view

before – poison. As clear now
as the wine-red smear stained on my lips,
left there by his. True love's kiss

does not look like this.
Nor the pale wrist, the twist
only offering the wrong side of the fruit.

The cottage: gone. The mountains: left.
And 7 men all bereft (I'm sure they wept)
no more fair maid to keep shut indoors;

'make the food', 'sweep the floors'. Bored.
The temptation understandable, given the context.
The apple so red, against the white. Bite

and release.
Breath, stale like death, revived.
Eyes stiff, winter white, open:

sharp crystal. Hammered home with gold,
a story told; of she who lies
and how she died. Looking out

the words reverse, patterns blurred
before the world, and me.
Reflections are a shocking thing,

once you realise what they truly mean.
I flex, try reach – feel the manacles of frozen wrists
shudder. I remember now,

how in each day of my sour slumber
the apple, lodged deep, turned. Knowledge
caught between throat and teeth and tongue

awake. I raise my head,
black hair a crown, ancestral wish.
I arm my jaw. Prepare to spit –

my story starts here:
lips drawn back

and the crack of gilded glass.

Look, how I took what you gave to me
rotten sharp weed. Read, how I held it,
choked it, out

and made my own seeds.

INBETWEEN TALES

When I was young,
I met a man who was a Jabberwock.
And in the parentheses of his smile
I grew, shrunk, twisted, changed.
I was frightened then.

Now I am old,
and fairy tales have no more meaning for me.
I have seen underneath the armour of knights,
and behind the wisdom of elders,
and found them
heavy and hollow.
My fears are different now.

I have lived my life in inbetweens,
half in and half out of the parentheses.
My tale is of one who kissed a toad
and found herself changed,
who hears its croak in place of her heartbeat.

I am wary of the children
who whisper stories by the fireside.
Scared they'll become changelings,
taken by the night.

ESTABLISHED 1978

I met a girl who had a laugh
that was two parts joy and one part childhood.
But now she has a chest so tight that she feels
that her ribs are holding her together
like a corset for the soul.

I don't believe that women were made from man's rib,
but I believe that her ribs have been bent
by the hands of man.
Made a cage rather than a crown
which she keeps hidden
behind a mickey mouse training bra, two vests,
and a baggy jumper.

I can see that the sleeves of her jumper are frayed, now
hurried to and fro between worrying hands
and clenched teeth.
She tells me she feels safer in her school uniform,
says to me that the men in the streets
and the buses
and the cars

and the trains
and the traffic lights
and the libraries
and the parks
and the bedrooms
are more likely to leave her alone.

Still, some get through, like nightmares do.

She says that her superpower is
that she can tell the sound of a man
without even looking up.
In fact, she is an expert at distinguishing
the subtle blend
of smell, sound, and shoe which means
she always knows
where they are,
and never has to look them in the eye.

I say to her your superpower is
every time you raise your head.

Your superpower is
every time you get out of bed,
and my heart
is broken for you.

I can't tell you the way
I'd like to hold you.
As you wish your mother had.
As I wish this world had.

But my rhymes

my rhymes are not enough.

And words don't come easy
in this language
of rape
            and survival.
And I have frays on my sleeves.
I know what it is
to learn
how to breathe.

THE ARCHIVIST

*After an illustration held in the Scottish Women's Aid
Archive, at Glasgow Women's Library, of a woman
with two lines drawn across her face.*

If she could give each line a name
she would say:

one, for me, for the years
for all I have been

and one, for him,
for the marks he left

which I am still easing.

THE YEARS

It was six years after the fact
that I became I
perhaps again, perhaps for the first time.

There was the suggestion
that I should mark each passage
with a commemoration
to what had been lost,
or survived,
words like redemption
but that was never I,
for I have nothing to apologise for
and I'll take my time.

Simply put,
the days followed the days
and the weeks followed the weeks
and the months the months
and the years the years
until I became I
until I became I.

LET ME TELL YOU

Let me tell you this:
I did not always look this way
and there were times
when you would not have recognised me.
I recognise you now.
I see you.

This road has been hard
and for you I won't lie
about the times of struggling –
suspicious of the walls
and wearing 'I'm fine' like a badge,
all the while hiding that beat beat beat in my chest,
I confess, I never felt less sane
than when his hand was clawing through my brain
and every man seemed to wear his face
and I thought, I might die tonight,
truly die tonight,
no one can sustain this.

So, you see,

it's hard to imagine one day you'll be living

when you're trying to survive.

Yet here I am.

And there you are.

I can't make any promises

or take it all away,

but, if you would like me to,

I can tell you, some things which I have learned:

That beat,

when you're terrified,

when it hurts,

when you think it can't get worse, *that* beat,

is a fight – but it's not the knife –

it's you.

It's you staying alive.

29

Congratulating me on turning twenty nine,
my friend tells me it's a number in its prime,
and I ask her what she means.

'It's only divisible by itself,'
she replies, and I nod,
and say, its about time,
my age finally reflected
who I am inside.

CHORUS

*A study released in 2016 by the University of Exeter found evidence
to suggest that female animals have adapted a subtler appearance
in order to avoid harassment from males.*

The scientists say women are evolving.
Say our drab mottled feathers, our scaled feet,
our lack of puff and shine and majesty
are deliberate.

We all know how it goes;
the slow glance across the watering hole
as he rests his pint on the bar,
opens his toothless beak,
and to his packmen tweets,
'that bird's a bit of alright.'

Later that night:
you trip among the groping of sharp bone
and web wings, membrane pulsing.

When you leave the floor
at the close of doors,

105

you hear a scuffle and a shout,
the cocky rings as the Blackbird sings
against the Rooster's caw:
'I saw ye lookin' at ma Hen', 'Ye saw me lookin' at yer Ma.'
Cock measuring. We all know, how it goes.

We are not alone.

Our sisters have been organising
for some time.
They have been trying to show us
their methods of resistance
to the Superb Bird of '*I'll show you Paradise*',
the *'do you come here often?'* of the Blue Manakin,
and the Long-Wattled Umbrellabird,
insisting he lives up to his name.

In solidarity, our sisters nest –
sharing tales of how they too have been pressed
against the puffed-up chest of the Andean
Cock-of-the-Rock
and a hard place.

Disgrace,
they know how it gets misplaced,
when you're told that you asked for it,

that your speckled brow drew in a crowd,
a redbreast above her station. Formation,
the scientists say, evolution and adaptation.

Ours has become weaponised, a response to the calls
of the prancing peacocks, even the proud lion's mane,
even the stag's horns, piercing the sky
like a promise that we, doe-eyed,
knew the answer to
long before we even recognised
that it could be a question.

The old drakes, white coats and boys only,
they thought our plain features and dowdy feet
were passive, to blend us in to habitats and homes.
Part of the furniture.

Among forest floors and cool algae ponds,
they had us sink,
hiding our young from the predators
who roam outside.

But, when we took the mantel,
and donned the white robe,
we recognised that the real predators
were the ones at home.

And so, we evolved.

Each scale harder, keener, resolute.

Each mossy feather concealing strong bone, honed
and ready.

We are the descendants of dinosaurs,

never forget:

our lineage draws back to ancient beasts,

the last living survivors of Theropod Queens.

Our evolution was deliberate.

Afraid of nothing.

And our young will live

to know.

GLOSSARY

As Salaam Alaikum – traditional greeting among Muslims, meaning 'may peace be upon you'. Can be said as a hello or goodbye.

Bali/Old Bali – Slang for father or old man, Zimbabwe, as taught to me by my old bali. The equivalent term for an older woman, mother (or in the poet's case, grand-mother) would be *Old Queen*.

Beta – Hindi term of endearment used towards a child. Traditionally used for boys, however can be used outwith this, as was in the Jassat family.

Cutri – Shortened version of 'Saala Cutra', drawn from Hindi phrase 'Saala Kutta', meaning roughly 'bloody dog'(old bali's translation). It is less clear if this adaptation is a formal change from the original (*kutta*, to *cutra*, to *cutri*) as cultures and languages migrated outside of India to Zimbabwe and Southern Africa, or if it is a specifically Jassat phenomenon.

Dua – Prayer, Islam. Also *Du'a*. Made by Auntie, every day.

Litchi – the spelling and pronunciation of Lychee used in Zimbabwe.

Lytie – slang for child/ young person, Zimbabwe, as taught by my old bali.

Owt, Nowt and *Sommet* – Yorkshire terms for 'anything', 'nothing' and 'something', respectively.

Roti – Bread. In the Jassat family, is specifically used to refer to circular flat bread.

Sadza – Maize meal dish, served in Zimbabwe, and at the Jassat dinner table.

Samoosa – alternative spelling and pronunciation of 'Samosa', Zimbabwe.

Snicket – a Northern English term for a narrow passage or alley.

Voetsek – Afrikaans term meaning to 'get lost'. Learned, with humour, via the old bali's use of it, especially when shouted at the TV.

Woe – a term used for burdensome relations; for example, 'in-laws' are often constructed or referred to in this way. As taught by the old bali, often met with a humorous eyeroll by my mother.

NOTES

The following poems first appeared in poetry pamphlet *Still* (Appletree Writers Press, 2016): 'Mother', 'Auntie', 'Girl Time', 'Inbetween Tales', 'Established 1978', 'The Years', 'Hopscotch', 'Braids', 'Let Me Tell You.' Minor variations may appear from the original pamphlet. 'Scot-Mid' was first published by the Dangerous Women Project on the 29th April 2016. Its form has been adapted from the original verse poem to the current version in this collection.

'The Gift' was first published online by the Hold My Purse Project, August 2017.

'Coin Toss (Heads/Tails)' was commissioned by StAnza International Poetry Festival, 2018. Supporting statistics can be found via the website for Women's Aid England and Wales, drawing on findings from Office of National Statistics as well as the Femicide Census (accurate as of Summer 2018.)

'Chorus' makes reference to icons in women's history and progress; Audre Lorde ('I am deliberate and afraid of nothing', *Sister Outsider,* 1984) and Beyonce's contemporary call to arms, 'Formation' (*Lemonade,* 2016). The study referred to in the poem is: *Why aren't signals of female quality more common?* by DJ Hosken, SH Alonzo and N Wedell, published in the scientific journal *Animal Behaviour,* March 2016.

'Braids' began in response to a task given in a writing workshop to write about the colour brown. The prompt was a quote from Michael Morpurgo writing in celebration of landscape and the colour brown, including the words: 'I live in a brown land which is turned and tilled … Brown is much maligned.' From: *Country Life Magazine,* 18th February 2015.

The poem referenced in 'Third Generation' is Langston Hughes' 'Cross' (*The Weary Blues,* 1927).

The signage referred to in 'Built to Last' was taken from the poet's notes following a visit to The British Museum in 2017, and the words 'hollow cast', 'seat cat', 'inlaid' and 'incised' are from the British Museum website, in reference to an object held on display.

'Sophie' quotes a line from the reported last words of Sophie Scholl. The full quote can be found widely online.

The opening quote from Gloria Anzaldua is taken from her wider statement: 'I will have my voice: Indian, Spanish, white. I will have my serpent's tongue – my woman's voice, my sexual voice, my poet's voice. I will overcome the tradition of silence.' ('How to Tame a Wild Tongue', in *Borderlands / La Frontera: The New Mestiza,* 1987).

ACKNOWLEDGEMENTS

Let Me Tell You This was a journey supported by many people close to my heart. Family, friends, helpers, healers, I trust you know who you are.

Thanks go to my mother. Many poems in this collection are to you, for you, inspired by you and the time we spend together – in particular 'Mother', one of the first poems I wrote after a long silence, and which sits like a land mark on this journey.

To my father – who only needs to look to the glossary, and his presence in it, to see the contribution he has made. Thank you for bringing the stories, food, and adventures which have been bridges of connection across time and geography.

Thank you to my brothers, Adam and Sameer, in particular Sameer for letting me share the poem I wrote about him with the world.

To Auntie Khutch, who read one of the many pieces about her and exclaimed with surprise, 'oh, it reminds me of me!'

To my cousin-sister Shereen, who has given me many

things, but in particular thank you for handing me a book which contained the following quote from Angela Davis: 'walls turned sideways are bridges.'

Thanks go to the many people who supported my career as a writer to date, including: Hannah Lavery of Appletree Writers; Heather McDaid and Laura Jones of 404 Ink; the wonderful staff and volunteers at Glasgow Women's Library, whose fierce championing of my work from the very beginning has been appreciated greatly; the Scottish Book Trust; The Edwin Morgan Trust; Sabrina Mahfouz; Kirsty Logan; Lena Wånggren for reading and feeding back on my writing with enthusiasm and attention to detail; Johanna Laitila and Zeba Talkhani for our respective writer chats.

Thanks to Roxana Vilk for her beautiful work on the film poem of 'Hopscotch'; Shazleen Khan for her stunning illustrations, the early drafts of which helped me resolve some of my own questions about the collection; Shagufta K Iqbal for bringing laughter into the editing process, knowing when to push, and knowing when to stay; and the many wonderful folk I have worked with in delivering creative writing workshops, for their openness, their honesty, and for sharing in this journey.

Thank you to James Barlow for his support, care, and acceptance; to my close colleagues in the movement to end gender-based violence, in particular those at the

Edinburgh Rape Crisis Centre, who brought support, encouragement, growth, and reminded me of the power of gentleness; and to those who accompanied me on my own journey, and helped me to realise my strength. Thank you.

I am grateful for the poets whose words found me at the right time, and the people who helped me find my words. My work is filled with voices, hands, words and hearts because these are the things from which my poetry is made. I would like to thank every person who has invested in, supported, and encouraged mine, and who has helped make me brave.

ABOUT THE AUTHOR

Nadine Aisha Jassat is an award-winning writer, poet, and creative practitioner.

She is the author of poetry pamphlet *Still* (Appletree Writers Press, 2016), editor of *Rise:* an anthology of writing from the young women's movement (YWCA Scotland, 2018), and her essays and short stories have been published widely online and in print, including in *New Writing Scotland*, The British Council's 'Discover' Project (for which she won the UK open call), Picador's *It's Not About the Burqa,* and 404 Ink's *Nasty Women.*

She is known for combining the creative arts with social justice, and her work has drawn significant acclaim: in 2018 she received a New Writers' Award from the Scottish Book Trust, as well as being short-listed for the Outspoken London Poetry Prize (Poetry in Film), and the prestigious Edwin Morgan Poetry Award. In 2017, she was named as one of 30 Inspiring Young Women Under 30 in Scotland.

Let Me Tell You This is her first full length collection.

The author photo features a spine poem (a poem made by the titles of books, as displayed on their spines) made by Nadine, as commissioned by the Scottish Book Trust in 2018. It reads:

Sister Outsider
Women of Resistance
Let Me Tell You This
We Shall Fight Until We Win.

I Am I Am I Am
The Woman Warrior
The Opposite of Fate
Part of My Soul
Surfacing
Finding A Voice
Falling Awake.

Little Women.
Nasty Women.
Bad Girls Throughout History.

The Things I Would Tell You.
Start Where You Are.
Speak.

ABOUT THE PUBLISHER

404 Ink is an independent, multi award-winning book and magazine publisher based in the UK, established in 2016. Led by two freelancers Laura Jones and Heather McDaid, their first commercial publication *Nasty Women*, a collection of essays and accounts on what it is to be a woman in the 21st century, garnered international praise from the likes of Margaret Atwood and Nicola Sturgeon and things have been going pretty well ever since.

Since then they have published the hilarious Chris McQueer, the enigmatic Helen McClory, New York Times bestseller Jason Reynolds, and more.

You can find out more at 404ink.com or follow them on Twitter, Facebook and Instagram by searching 404 Ink.

If you enjoyed

LET ME TELL YOU THIS

you may also like...

Nasty Women

A collection of essays and accounts on what it is to be a woman in the 21st century.

'An essential window into many of the hazard-strewn worlds younger women are living in right now'
– Margaret Atwood

We Shall Fight Until We Win

A graphic anthology celebrating a century of pioneering women, marking the centenary of the first wave of women gaining the right to vote in the UK.

'Beautiful and inspiring'
– Laura Bates
'Compulsive reading' – Stylist

For Every One
by Jason Reynolds
(co-publication with Knights Of)

FOR EVERY ONE is for every kind of reader. A letter to anyone who has ever had a keep-you-up-at-night ambition. The heart racing, what if? This book is a challenge to think beyond the expected and go for what you want, when going for it is the scariest part. An ideal gift for anyone from a school leaver to a retiree, for the creative, ambitious or those going on an adventure.

'Defiant and inspirational' – The Guardian

All of these books can be purchased on:

404ink.com/shop